The Anne of Green Gables Cookbook

The Anne of Green Gables Cookbook

Charming Recipes
from Anne and Her Friends in Avonlea

Kate Macdonald
AND L.M. MONTGOMERY

Race Point
PUBLISHING

First published in 2017 by Race Point Publishing, an imprint of The Quarto Group,
142 West 36th Street, 4th Floor, New York, NY 10018, USA
T (212) 779-4972 **F** (212) 779-6058 **www.Quarto.com**

Published with permission by the Heirs of L.M. Montgomery Inc. This is a revised and expanded edition of
The Anne of Green Gables Cookbook published in 1985 by Oxford University Press.

Race Point titles are also available at discount for retail, wholesale, promotional, and bulk purchase. For
details, contact the Special Sales Manager by email at specialsales@quarto.com or by mail at The Quarto Group,
Attn: Special Sales Manager, 100 Cummings Center Suite 265D, Beverly, MA 01915, USA.

20 19 18 17 16 15 14 13

ISBN: 978-1-63106-374-9

Library of Congress Cataloging-in-Publication Data

Names: Macdonald, Kate, author.
Title: The Anne of Green Gables cookbook : charming recipes from Anne and her
    friends in Avonlea / Kate Macdonald.
Description: New York, NY, USA : Race Point Publishing, an imprint of The
    Quarto Group, [2017] | Includes index.
Identifiers: LCCN 2017023425 | ISBN 9781631063749 (hardcover)
Subjects: LCSH: Cooking--Juvenile literature. | Montgomery, L. M. (Lucy
    Maud), 1874-1942. Anne of Green Gables. | LCGFT: Literary Cookbooks.
Classification: LCC TX652.5 .M245 2017 | DDC 641.5--dc23 LC record available at https://lccn.loc.gov/2017023425

Editorial Director: Jeannine Dillon
Creative Director: Merideth Harte
Managing Editor: Erin Canning
Photography: Evi Abeler
Food Stylist: Michaela Hayes
Photography and Food Stylist Intern: Alyssa Kondracki
Cover and Interior Design: Merideth Harte
Props provided by Karen Smith-Canning

Printed in China

In memory of my mom and dad.

Contents

RECIPES FROM ANNE OF GREEN GABLES

RECIPES FROM ANNE OF AVONLEA

RECIPES FROM ANNE OF WINDY POPLARS

RECIPES FROM L.M. MONTGOMERY'S KITCHEN

Introduction

Marilla is right, you must keep your wits about you in the kitchen. Anne eventually became a good cook following Marilla's advice, and you can, too. By reading the recipes carefully and following the directions, you'll be able to turn out delicious treats for yourself, your friends, and your family.

Keep your wits about you, and keep these general suggestions in mind before you start:

- Check with the grown-ups in the house to make sure you'll be using the kitchen at a convenient time.

- Some kitchen equipment can be dangerous if used improperly. If you don't know how to use a piece of equipment, ask your parents or someone with experience for help or advice.

- Read the recipe two or three times before you begin—just to make sure you understand what you are supposed to do. If there's anything you don't understand, don't be afraid to ask.

- Always start with clean hands.

Now you're ready to begin. It's a good idea to gather all the utensils and ingredients before you start cooking. That way you won't have to stop in the middle to look for things.

There are explanations of cooking terms and some useful cooking tipson pages 15 and 16, and all the recipes are arranged to make cooking easy. There's no secret to being a good cook if you do what the recipe says. I know all the recipes work because I have tested them. They are all delicious, so I'm sure that whatever you try will be as well.

When this original collection of recipes was first published in 1985, it was before I had children of my own. I now understand more clearly how much pleasure comes from providing good, tasty food. The recipes in the original collection were inspired by passages from the Anne books, specifically *Anne of Green Gables, Anne of Avonlea,* and *Anne of Windy Poplars.* Those recipes are included here along with eleven new ones: some are inspired by the previously mentioned books and others are from L.M. Montgomery's own kitchen. L.M. Montgomery was my grandmother and she loved cooking. I adapted her recipes to make them easier for you.

My grandmother also enjoyed cooking for her family, and according to my father, Stuart, she was a sensational cook. When she wasn't too busy with her writing, she thoroughly enjoyed providing delicious treats for her husband, Ewan, and her two sons, Stuart and Chester.

There are a few safety hints you ought to remember:

- When using vegetable peelers or knives, always cut away from yourself so you won't cut your hands.

- When using saucepans, always turn the handles toward the back of the stove so that nobody will bump into them and knock over the hot contents.

- And, always make sure you turn off the stove when you're finished.

Last, but not least, if you want to be welcome in the kitchen, be sure to leave it exactly as you found it. Keep your work surfaces clean so you can see what you're doing! Clean up any spills as you go along. And while you're waiting for something to cook, it's a good idea to wash the dishes you've already used. This way, you won't have such a big job to do at the end. My dad used to say, "Clean as you go, Katie, clean as you go." If you keep these suggestions and hints in mind and remember what Marilla said, you'll turn out to be just as good a cook as Anne eventually was. And you'll have lots of fun pleasing your friends and family for years to come.

Bon appétit!

Cooking Tips

Getting Started

- Read the recipe 2 or 3 times.

- Gather all the ingredients and equipment. Some recipes have a "You Will Need" section that lists special kitchen equipment needed for the recipe.

- Make sure you have a clean and organized work space, along with clean hands.

- Thoroughly wash all produce before using.

- Ask a grown-up any questions you may have.

Eggs

Adding eggs: When adding eggs to any recipe, first break them into a separate bowl. If any shells fall into the eggs, you can remove them easily—so they won't end up in the recipe!

Separating eggs: To separate eggs, use 2 small bowls. Crack the egg on the rim of one of the bowls. Pull the shell apart and hold the yolk in one half of the shell. Let the white dribble into one bowl, then tip the yolk into the other half of the shell. Let the rest of the white dribble into the bowl. Put the yolk in the second bowl.

Frosting

When frosting a layer cake, always make sure to turn the bottom layer over so that its top side is facedown. After you frost the bottom layer, put the top layer on—right side up—and frost it. This way, you'll have 2 flat sides in the middle of your cake—and you won't find the top layer sliding off!

Measuring

Butter or shortening: Press it firmly into a measuring cup or spoon until there are no air pockets.

Brown sugar: Always pack it very firmly into a dry measuring cup or spoon.

Flour and dry ingredients: Pile them gently into a dry measuring cup or spoon, then level them off with a metal spatula or knife.

Liquid ingredients: If using a liquid measuring cup, set the measuring cup on the counter and fill it up to the amount you need. To check your measuring, bend down until your eye is level with the desired amount.

Testing

To test a cake for doneness, insert a toothpick into the center. If it comes out clean, it is done. If cake clings to the toothpick, shut the oven door and test it again in 5 minutes.

Cooking Terms

Boil
Heat a liquid on the stove over high heat until it bubbles.

Cream
Beat a mixture of butter or shortening and sugar with an electric mixer until it is smooth and creamy.

Cut In
Add butter or shortening to a flour mixture and cut it with a pastry blender or 2 knives until the pieces are the size called for in the recipe.

Flour
To flour pans after greasing them, sprinkle a little extra flour into the pans and shake them until the whole surface is covered. Shake out any excess flour.

Fold
With a rubber spatula, cut gently down through the mixture, then along the bottom of the bowl, and then up and over in a circular motion. Turn the bowl and repeat until the mixture is gently blended.

Grate
Scrape an ingredient against the holes of a grater, to make small pieces or shreds.

Grease
To grease a baking pan or dish, hold a small piece of butter in a bit of paper towel or wax paper and rub the butter all over the inside of the pan or dish.

Knead
Put the heels of your hands on the dough. Push the dough down and away from you. Fold the dough in half and push down and away again, then turn the dough one-quarter of a turn each time you push, until every part of the dough is kneaded.

Poach
To cook in a hot liquid that is kept just below the boiling point.

Preheat
Turn on the oven to the degree given in the recipe. Let the oven reach this temperature before you bake.

Sift
To remove lumps, place dry ingredients through a sifter, then measure the amount you need.

Simmer
Cook a mixture just below the boiling point. A few bubbles will form slowly and burst before they come to the top.

Steam
Cook food on a rack in a covered pot over simmering water.

RECIPES FROM
Anne of Green Gables

Puffy APPLE DUMPLINGS

Prep time: 30 minutes **Total time:** 1 hour 10 minutes **Yield:** 6 dumplings

> "The 'Avenue' . . . was a stretch of road four or five hundred yards long, completely arched over with huge, wide-spreading apple-trees, planted years ago by an eccentric old farmer. Overhead was one long canopy of snowy, fragrant bloom. . . . 'They should call it—let me see— the White Way of Delight.'"
>
> —Anne Shirley, CHAPTER II

INGREDIENTS

Dough
1½ cups (180 g) all-purpose flour, plus more for work surface and rolling pin
3 teaspoons baking powder
½ teaspoon salt
5 tablespoons (75 g) butter
½ cup (120 ml) 2% milk

Filling
6 small apples, peeled, cored, and sliced
6 teaspoons sugar, plus more for sprinkling
1½ teaspoons butter, plus more for dotting
Ground cinnamon, for sprinkling

1. Preheat the oven to 400°F (200°C).

2. **To make the dough:** Sift the flour, baking powder, and salt into a medium mixing bowl.

3. Mix in the butter with your fingers until it is well distributed. Add the milk to make a soft dough.

4. Turn the dough out onto a lightly floured board or countertop. Flour a rolling pin and roll out the dough, about ¼ inch (6 mm) thick. Divide the dough into 6 equal pieces.

5. **To make the filling:** On each dough piece, place some sliced apples, pressing them tightly together, then add 1 teaspoon sugar and ¼ teaspoon butter.

6. With fingers dipped in water, moisten the edges of the dough and fold it up around the apple filling. Place the dumplings on an ungreased baking sheet.

7. Sprinkle each dumpling with cinnamon and sugar, and dot with more butter.

8. Bake for 40 minutes until golden brown. Use oven mitts to remove the baking sheet from the oven and set on a cooling rack.

9. Serve warm and enjoy with the Light and Creamy Vanilla Ice Cream (page 26) or Caramel Pudding Sauce (page 40).

Chocolate CARAMELS

Prep time: 45 minutes **Total time:** 2 hours 15 minutes (includes cooling) **Yield:** 10 caramels

" 'I had one chocolate caramel once two years ago and it was simply delicious. I've often dreamed since then that I had a lot of chocolate caramels, but I always wake up just when I'm going to eat them.' "

—Anne Shirley, CHAPTER III

INGREDIENTS

1 cup (2 sticks, or 240 g) unsalted butter, plus more for greasing

3 ounces (85 g) semi-sweet chocolate

1¼ cups (380 g) sweetened condensed milk

¼ cup (80 g) corn syrup

2¼ cups (495 g) firmly packed brown sugar

You Will Need
* 8 x 8-inch (20 x 20 cm) baking pan

This recipe requires lots of patience during the cooking time, but it's well worth it!

1. Grease an 8 x 8-inch (20 x 20 cm) baking pan with butter. Set it aside.

2. Add the butter, chocolate, sweetened condensed milk, corn syrup, and brown sugar to a large heavy saucepan. Mix with a wooden spoon.

3. Place the saucepan over medium heat and let the mixture come to a boil. Let the chocolate melt completely.

4. Reduce the heat to medium-low and cook the mixture for 30 minutes. It should boil gently during this time. With the wooden spoon, stir the mixture constantly the entire time. It's important to stir constantly because candy burns easily.

5. When it's cooked, the candy will be very thick. Pour it into the baking pan and set it on a cooling rack.

6. Let the candy cool completely, about 1½ hours, then cut it into ¾-inch (2 cm) squares.

Sunshiny CORN SOUFFLÉ

—

Prep time: 20 minutes **Total time:** 1 hour **Yield:** 4 to 6 servings

" 'The world doesn't seem such a howling wilderness as it did last night. I'm so glad it's a sunshiny morning.' "

—Anne Shirley, CHAPTER IV

INGREDIENTS

¼ cup (½ stick, or 60 g) butter, plus more
   for greasing
¼ cup (30 g) all-purpose flour
⅔ cup (160 ml) milk
½ cup (60 g) grated Cheddar cheese
1 tablespoon (10 g) minced green bell
   pepper
1 can (11 ounces, or 311 g) corn
   niblets, drained
3 eggs

You Will Need
• Small casserole or baking dish
• Electric mixer

1. Preheat the oven to 300°F (150°C). Grease a small casserole dish with butter. Set it aside.

2. Add the butter and flour to a medium saucepan. Cook and stir over low heat until all the flour is absorbed. Add the milk and continue cooking and stirring until the sauce thickens. Remove from the heat. Add the grated cheese, green pepper, and corn to the sauce. Combine. Set aside.

3. Break the eggs and separate the yolks and whites into 2 small bowls. Mix the egg yolks into the sauce.

4. Beat the egg whites with an electric mixer until soft peaks form. Fold them into the sauce.

5. Transfer the mixture to the greased casserole dish.

6. Bake for 30 to 40 minutes, until the mixture sets like custard. Use oven mitts to remove the dish from the oven.

7. Serve immediately.

Light and Creamy VANILLA ICE CREAM

Prep time: 50 minutes **Total time:** 3 hours 50 minutes (includes freezing) **Yield:** 4 to 6 servings

" 'I have never tasted ice cream. Diana tried to explain what it was like, but I guess ice cream is one of those things that are beyond imagination.' "

—Anne Shirley, CHAPTER XIII

INGREDIENTS

2 cups (475 ml) whipping cream
2 teaspoons gelatin
¼ cup (60 ml) cold water
1 cup (235 ml) 2% or whole milk
½ cup (100 g) sugar
3 tablespoons (65 g) corn syrup
1 teaspoon all-purpose flour
Pinch salt
1 large egg
1 tablespoon (15 ml) pure vanilla extract

You Will Need
- Electric mixer
- Double boiler

This ice cream is deliciously light and creamy.

1. Place the whipping cream, electric beaters, and a large mixing bowl in the refrigerator to chill.

2. Add about 2 inches (5 cm) of water to the bottom pot of a double boiler and bring to a boil.

3. Add the gelatin and cold water to the top pot of the double boiler. Let the gelatin soften for 5 minutes away from the stove.

4. Meanwhile, pour the milk into a small saucepan and place it over medium-low heat. When tiny bubbles form around the edge of the pot, the milk is ready.

5. To the gelatin in the top pot of the double boiler, add the hot milk, sugar, corn syrup, flour, and salt. Place over the bottom pot of the double boiler containing the boiling water.

6. Stir constantly with a wooden spoon until the mixture thickens, about 15 minutes.

7. Put the lid on the double boiler and cook the mixture over boiling water for another 10 minutes.

8. Meanwhile, break the egg and separate the yolk and white into 2 small mixing bowls. Set aside the egg white for later.

9. Beat the egg yolk *slightly* with a fork. When the 10 minutes are up, stir the egg yolk *very slowly* into the mixture on top of the stove. Cook and stir for 1 more minute.

10. Pour the hot ice cream mixture through a wire strainer into a large mixing bowl (not the chilled one).

11. When the ice cream mixture has cooled to room temperature, beat it with the electric mixer until it is light and creamy, about 5 minutes.

12. In the chilled large mixing bowl, whip the cold whipping cream with the electric mixer and chilled beaters until it falls in large globs and forms a soft peak.

13. Rinse the beaters thoroughly with hot water, then beat the egg white until it is stiff and glossy but not dry.

14. Very gently, with a rubber spatula, fold first the whipped cream, then the egg white, into the ice cream mixture. Gently stir in the vanilla extract.

15. Spoon the mixture into a metal bowl or pan and place in the freezer. Freeze for about 3 or 4 hours, until firm.

16. Eat by itself or serve with the Puffy Apple Dumplings (page 21); see ice cream in that photo for reference).

" 'And we had the ice cream. Words fail me to describe that ice cream. Marilla, I assure you it was sublime.' "

—Anne Shirely, CHAPTER XIV

𝒯antalizing **RASPBERRY TARTS**

Prep time: 50 minutes **Total time**: 1 hour 30 minutes (includes cooling) **Yield**: 12 tarts

"The little girls of Avonlea School always pooled their lunches, and to eat three raspberry tarts all alone or even to share them only with one's best chum would have forever and ever branded as 'awful mean' the girl who did it. And yet, when the tarts were divided among ten girls you just got enough to tantalize you."

—CHAPTER XV

INGREDIENTS
Crust
1 cup (120 g) all-purpose flour
1 tablespoon (15 ml) sugar
¼ teaspoon salt
6 tablespoons (90 g) cold butter
1 large egg
1 tablespoon (15 ml) water
1 tablespoon (15 ml) lemon juice

1. Preheat the oven to 425°F (220°C).

2. **To make the crust:** Add the flour, sugar, and salt to a large mixing bowl. Combine. With a pastry blender, cut in the cold butter until the mixture looks like tiny peas.

3. Break the egg and separate the egg yolk and white into 2 small bowls. To the egg yolk, add the water and the lemon juice. Mix with a fork. (You can use the egg white in another recipe or discard.)

4. Sprinkle the egg yolk mixture over the flour mixture. Stir with the fork until the pastry holds together in a ball.

5. With your fingers, pull small pieces of pastry from the ball and press them evenly against the bottom and sides of each tart tin. The pastry should be about ⅛ inch (3 mm) thick. Refrigerate the tart shells while you make the filling.

6. **To make the filling:** Add the cornstarch and water to a small saucepan. Mix with a wooden spoon until smooth. Stir in the sugar. Add the thawed raspberries to the saucepan. Cook over medium-low heat until thick, 10 to 15 minutes. Let the mixture cool.

7. Spoon the raspberry filling evenly into each tart shell, no more than two-thirds full.

continued

Filling

3 tablespoons (22 g) cornstarch
¼ cup (60 ml) water
¾ cup (150 g) sugar
1 package (10 ounces, or 284 g) frozen
  unsweetened raspberries, thawed, or 2⅓
  cups (285 g) fresh raspberries

You Will Need

- Twelve 3-inch (7.5 cm) tart tins or
  12-cup muffin tin

8. Bake the tarts for 10 minutes, then turn down the oven to 350°F (180°C) and bake them for 15 minutes more, or until they are golden brown.

9. Use oven mitts to remove the tarts from the oven and set them on a cooling rack. Let them cool for 15 minutes, then gently remove them from the tins.

Gilbert's **HURRY-UP DINNER**

—

Prep time: 10 minutes **Total time:** 50 minutes (includes making mashed potatoes) **Yield:** 4 servings

" 'I think your Gilbert Blythe *is* handsome,' confided Anne to Diana, 'But I think he's very bold. It isn't good manners to wink at a strange girl.' "

—CHAPTER XV

1. Add the butter to a medium saucepan and melt over medium heat, then add the flour. When all the flour is mixed in, add the milk.

2. Add the salt, black pepper, and frozen peas to the pan. Cook until the mixture thickens.

3. Add the salmon to the pan, breaking it up into pieces. Once the salmon is warmed, remove from the heat.

4. Serve with the mashed potatoes and top with chopped parsley, if using.

INGREDIENTS

3 tablespoons (45 g) butter
¼ cup (30 g) all-purpose flour
2½ cups (600 ml) 2% milk
½ teaspoon salt
Black pepper, to taste
1 cup (150 g) frozen peas
7 ounces (198 g) canned salmon or tuna, drained
Mashed potatoes, for serving (see Rachel Lynde's North Shore Fish Cakes on page 92 for the recipe)
Chopped parsley, for topping (optional)

Maritime GINGERSNAPS

—

Prep time: 1 hour **Total time:** 1 hour 30 minutes **Yield:** about 48 cookies

" 'You'll put down the old brown tea set. But you can open the little yellow crock of cherry preserves. It's time it was being used anyhow—I believe it's beginning to go. And you can cut some fruit-cake and have some of the cookies and snaps.' "

—Marilla Cuthbert, CHAPTER XVI

INGREDIENTS

½ cup (100 g) sugar
½ cup (170 g) molasses
¼ cup (48 g) vegetable shortening
1½ cups (180 g) all-purpose flour
¼ teaspoon baking powder
2 teaspoons ground ginger
1 teaspoon ground cinnamon
1 teaspoon ground cloves
¼ teaspoon salt

1. Place the oven racks in the center of the oven. Preheat the oven to 375°F (190°C). Line cookie sheets with parchment paper.

2. Add the sugar, molasses, and shortening to a small saucepan. With a wooden spoon, stir over medium heat until it reaches the boiling point. Immediately remove from the heat and let cool.

3. Add the flour, baking powder, ginger, cinnamon, cloves, and salt to a large mixing bowl. Mix together.

4. When the molasses mixture is cool, pour it over the flour mixture. Mix well. Chill the dough in the refrigerator for about 10 minutes.

5. Shape the dough into small balls—about the size of a quarter—and arrange them 2 inches (5 cm) apart on cookie sheets. Flatten the balls with the bottom of a small drinking glass or with your fingers.

6. Bake the gingersnaps until crispy and dry, 6 to 8 minutes. Watch them closely—they can burn very easily.

7. Use oven mitts to remove the cookie sheets from the oven. Set the sheets on a cooling rack. Let the gingersnaps cool for 5 minutes, then lift them from the cookie sheet with a metal spatula.

Diana Barry's Favorite RASPBERRY CORDIAL

Prep time: 40 minutes **Total time:** 2 hours (includes cooling) **Yield:** 4 to 6 servings

> "Diana poured herself out a tumblerful, looked at its bright-red hue admiringly, and then sipped it daintily."
>
> **—CHAPTER XVI**

INGREDIENTS

2 packages (10 ounces, or 284 g, each)
   frozen unsweetened raspberries
1¼ cups (250 g) sugar
3 lemons, divided
4 cups (950 ml) water

This recipe for raspberry cordial will never be confused with Marilla's "three-year-old homemade currant wine for which she is celebrated in Avonlea."

1. Put the unthawed raspberries into a large saucepan and add the sugar.

2. Cook over medium heat, stirring occasionally, for 20 to 25 minutes, until all the sugar has dissolved.

3. With a potato masher, mash the raspberries and syrup thoroughly.

4. Pour the mixture through a strainer, making sure you extract all of the juice. Discard the pulp.

5. Squeeze 2 of the lemons and strain the juice. Add the juice to the raspberry liquid.

6. Bring the water to a boil, then add the boiling water to the raspberry liquid.

7. Let the raspberry cordial cool, then chill it in the refrigerator.

8. When the cordial is ready to serve, cut the remaining lemon into thin slices and float a slice in each glass.

Marilla's **PLUM PUDDING**

—

Prep time: 40 minutes **Total time:** 4 hours (includes cooling) **Yield:** 6 to 8 servings

" 'Diana, fancy if you can my extreme horror at finding a mouse drowned in that pudding sauce!' "

—Anne Shirley, CHAPTER XVI

INGREDIENTS

Plum Pudding

1 stick (½ cup, or 120 g) butter, plus more for greasing

½ cup (100 g) sugar, plus more for sprinkling

½ cup (75 g) raisins

½ cup (75 g) currants

1 cup (120 g) all-purpose flour, plus more for sprinkling

½ cup (75 g) fresh breadcrumbs

½ teaspoon baking powder

½ teaspoon salt

½ teaspoon ground cinnamon

½ teaspoon ground nutmeg

¼ cup (40 g) chopped walnuts

½ cup (120 ml) milk

1 large egg

¼ cup (85 g) molasses

Some boiling water

1. **To make the plum pudding:** Grease the pudding mold or bowl with butter, then sprinkle it with a bit of extra sugar. Shake the mold until the inside surface is covered with sugar. Set it aside.

2. Chop the raisins and currants with a knife. Sprinkle them with a little of the extra flour and set them aside.

3. Add the 1 cup (120 g) flour, ½ cup (100 g) sugar, breadcrumbs, baking powder, salt, cinnamon, and nutmeg to a large bowl. Mix with a wooden spoon.

4. With a pastry blender, cut in the butter until the mixture looks like coarse breadcrumbs. Add the chopped raisins, currants, and walnuts to the flour mixture. Mix with the wooden spoon.

5. Pour the milk into a small saucepan and place it over low heat. When tiny bubbles form around the edge of the pot, the milk is ready. Remove from the heat.

6. Break the egg into the small bowl, then add it to the fruit-and-flour mixture. Add the hot milk and molasses. With the wooden spoon, mix everything well.

7. Spoon the mixture into the pudding mold or 1-quart (1 L) bowl. Make a cover for the mold with 2 layers of aluminum foil, and butter the side of the foil that will lie against the pudding. Tie string around the foil cover to keep it tight.

☞ continued

Caramel Pudding Sauce

½ cup (115 g) firmly packed
   brown sugar
1½ tablespoons (23 ml) flour
Pinch salt
1 cup (235 ml) boiling water
½ teaspoon vanilla extract
1 tablespoon (15 g) butter

You Will Need

- Pudding mold or 1-quart
  (1 L) bowl
- String
- Canning rack or Mason-
  jar ring

8. Set a canning rack or Mason-jar ring in a large pot. Set the covered pudding on top. Carefully pour some boiling water down the side of the large pot until it comes halfway up the pudding mold. Bring the large pot to a boil. Reduce the heat to medium-low and cover with the lid. (If needed, add more water during the cooking.)

9. Steam the pudding for 3 hours. Insert a clean toothpick into the center of the pudding (right through the foil). If it comes out clean, the pudding is done. If pudding clings to the toothpick, check again in 15 minutes.

10. Preheat the oven on a low heat. When the pudding is done, use oven mitts to remove it from the large pot. Remove the foil and let the pudding stand for 10 minutes. Warm a platter in the oven.

11. Turn the pudding upside down onto a warm platter.

12. **To make the caramel pudding sauce:** Combine the brown sugar, flour, and salt in a small saucepan. Very gradually add the boiling water and stir with a wooden spoon. Over low heat, stir the mixture until it is thick and creamy, about 5 minutes.

13. When the sauce is thick, remove the saucepan from the heat. Stir in the butter and vanilla extract. Let the butter melt completely.

14. Serve warm over Marilla's Plum Pudding. If you have any pudding sauce left over, don't forget—like Anne did—to cover it tightly.

Chocolate Goblin's **FOOD CAKE**

—

Prep time: 1 hour **Total time:** 3 hours (includes cooling and frosting) **Yield:** 6 to 8 servings

" 'I just grow cold when I think of my layer cake. Oh, Diana, what if it shouldn't be good! I dreamed last night that I was chased all around by a fearful goblin with a big layer cake for a head.' "

—Anne Shirley, CHAPTER XXI

INGREDIENTS

Chocolate Goblin's Food Cake
¾ cup (1½ sticks, or 180g) butter, melted, plus more for greasing
1¾ cups (190 g) sifted all-purpose flour, plus more for the pans
1 cup (235 ml) water
4 ounces (113 g) unsweetened chocolate
1½ teaspoons baking soda
½ teaspoon baking powder
1 teaspoon salt
1½ cups (300 g) granulated sugar
1 cup (235 ml) 2% milk
3 large eggs
1 teaspoon pure vanilla extract

1. Arrange the oven racks so that the cakes will sit in the center of the oven. Preheat the oven to 350°F (180°C). Grease two 9-inch (23 cm) cake pans with butter, then flour the pans. Set them aside.

2. **To make the cake:** In a small saucepan, bring the water to a boil. Set a small metal or heatproof mixing bowl over the boiling water and add the chocolate. Reduce the heat to low and melt the chocolate. Remove the small bowl from the heat and let it cool. You can also use a double boiler. See step 11 on page 42 for instructions.

3. Add the sifted flour, baking soda, baking powder, salt, and sugar to a large mixing bowl. Mix with a wooden spoon.

4. Add the melted chocolate, milk, and melted butter to the flour mixture. Mix with the wooden spoon, then beat for 1 minute with an electric mixer.

5. Break the eggs into a small bowl. Add the eggs and vanilla extract to the cake batter. Beat with the mixer for another 3 minutes, constantly scraping down the sides of the bowl with rubber spatula.

6. Pour the cake batter evenly into the 2 cake pans. Bake the cakes for 30 to 35 minutes.

continued

Chocolate Fudge Frosting

2 cups (360 g) semi-sweet chocolate chips
¼ cup (48 g) vegetable shortening
2½ cups (320 g) confectioners' sugar
½ cup (60 ml) milk

You Will Need

- Two 9-inch (23 cm) round cake pans
  Electric mixer
- 2 cooling racks
- Double boiler (optional)

7. Test the cakes with a toothpick. When they are done, use oven mitts to remove them from the oven. Let them cool in the pans for 10 minutes.

8. Slide the blade of a metal spatula around the edges of the cakes to loosen them from the pans.

9. Place one of the cakes on a cooling rack. Place a second cooling rack on top. Hold the 2 racks and flip the whole thing over. The cake is now upside-down on the rack. Gently lift off the pan and transfer your cake to a plate. Repeat with the other cake.

10. Let the 2 layers cool completely before frosting.

11. **To make the frosting:** Put 2 inches (5 cm) of water in the bottom of the double boiler and bring to a simmer. Add the chocolate chips and the vegetable shortening to the top pot of a double boiler. Set it over the simmering water and let the chocolate chips and the shortening melt. If you don't have a double boiler, you can use a saucepan and a metal or heatproof mixing bowl. See step 2 on page 41 for instructions.

12. Stir in the confectioners' sugar, a little at a time, with a wooden spoon. Add the milk. Remove the top pot from the heat.

13. Beat the frosting with the electric mixer until it is thick and creamy, about 5 minutes.

14. With a metal spatula, spread about one-third of the frosting between the 2 layers of the cake and use the rest to cover the top and sides, if desired, of your cake. If you rinse the metal spatula under hot water from time to time while frosting the cake, the frosting will spread more easily. See page 15 for frosting tips

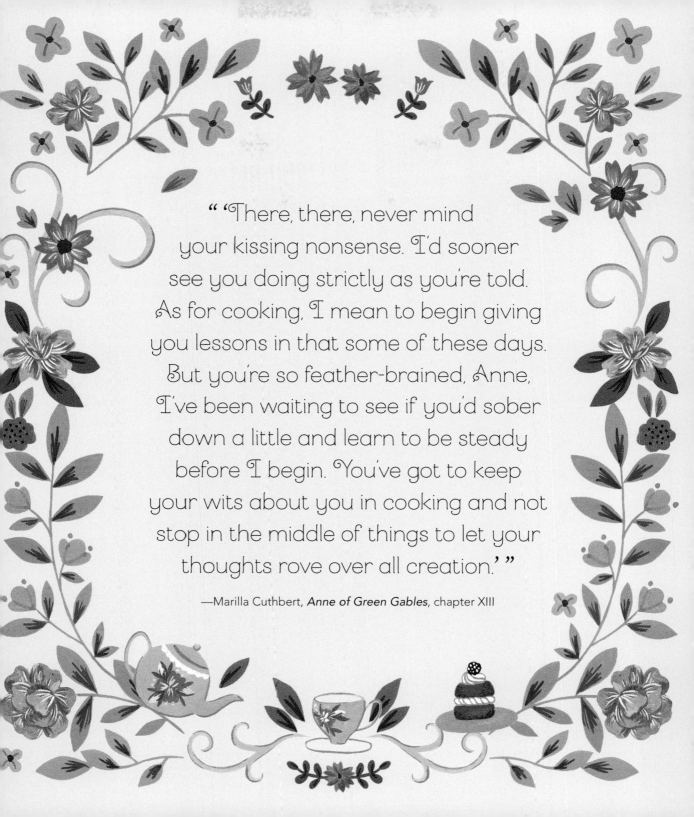

" "There, there, never mind your kissing nonsense. I'd sooner see you doing strictly as you're told. As for cooking, I mean to begin giving you lessons in that some of these days. But you're so feather-brained, Anne, I've been waiting to see if you'd sober down a little and learn to be steady before I begin. You've got to keep your wits about you in cooking and not stop in the middle of things to let your thoughts rove over all creation.' "

—Marilla Cuthbert, *Anne of Green Gables*, chapter XIII

Anne's LINIMENT CAKE

Prep time: 30 minutes **Total time:** 2 hours 30 minutes (includes cooling and frosting) **Yield:** 6 to 8 servings

> " 'Mercy on us, Anne, you've flavored that cake with *Anodyne Liniment*. I broke the liniment bottle last week and poured what was left into an old empty vanilla bottle. I suppose it's partly my fault—I should have warned you—but for pity's sake, why couldn't you have smelled it?' "
>
> —Marilla Cuthbert, CHAPTER XXI

INGREDIENTS
Liniment Cake
½ cup (1 stick, or 120 g) butter, melted, plus more for greasing
2 cups (220 g) sifted all-purpose flour, plus more for the pans
1 tablespoon (15 ml) baking powder
Pinch salt
1¼ cups (250 g) granulated sugar
1 cup (235 ml) 2% milk
3 large eggs
2 teaspoons pure vanilla extract

Here's the cake Anne really meant to make. Be sure you use vanilla extract—not anodyne liniment!

1. Arrange the oven racks so that the cakes will sit in the center of the oven. Preheat the oven to 350°F (180°C). Grease two 9-inch (23 cm) cake pans with butter, then flour the pans. Set them aside.

2. **To make the cake:** Add the flour, baking powder, salt, and sugar to a large bowl. Mix together.

3. Add the melted butter and the milk to the flour mixture and stir with a wooden spoon.

4. Beat the mixture for 1 minute with an electric mixer.

5. Break the eggs into a small bowl. Add the eggs and vanilla extract, to the cake batter, then beat with the mixer for another 3 minutes, constantly scraping down the sides of the bowl with a rubber spatula.

6. Pour the cake batter evenly into the 2 cake pans. Bake for 25 to 30 minutes.

7. Test the cakes with a toothpick. When they are done, use oven mitts to remove them from the oven. Let them cool in the pans for 10 minutes.

8. Slide the blade of a metal spatula around the edges of the cakes to loosen them from the pans.

 continued

46

Creamy Butter Frosting

1 cup (2 sticks, or 240 g) unsalted butter, softened

3 cups (360 g) confectioners' sugar

⅛ teaspoon salt

1½ teaspoons pure vanilla extract

3 tablespoons (45 ml) heavy cream

2 or 3 drops red food coloring (optional)

You Will Need

- Two 9-inch (23 cm) round cake pans
- Electric mixer
- 2 cooling racks

9. Place one of the cakes on a cooling rack. Place a second cooling rack on top. Hold the 2 racks together and flip the whole thing over. The cake is now upside-down on the rack. Gently lift off the pan and transfer your cake to a plate. Repeat with the other cake.

10. Let the 2 layers cool completely before frosting with the Creamy Butter Frosting.

11. **To make the frosting:** Cream the softened butter with an electric mixer.

12. Gradually add the confectioners' sugar until it is all combined.

13. Mix in the salt, vanilla extract, cream, and food coloring. Beat on low speed with an electric mixer for 10 minutes, until frosting is silky.

14. With a metal spatula, spread about one-third of the frosting between the 2 cake layers Use the remaining two-thirds to cover the top and sides of your cake. See page 15 for frosting tips.

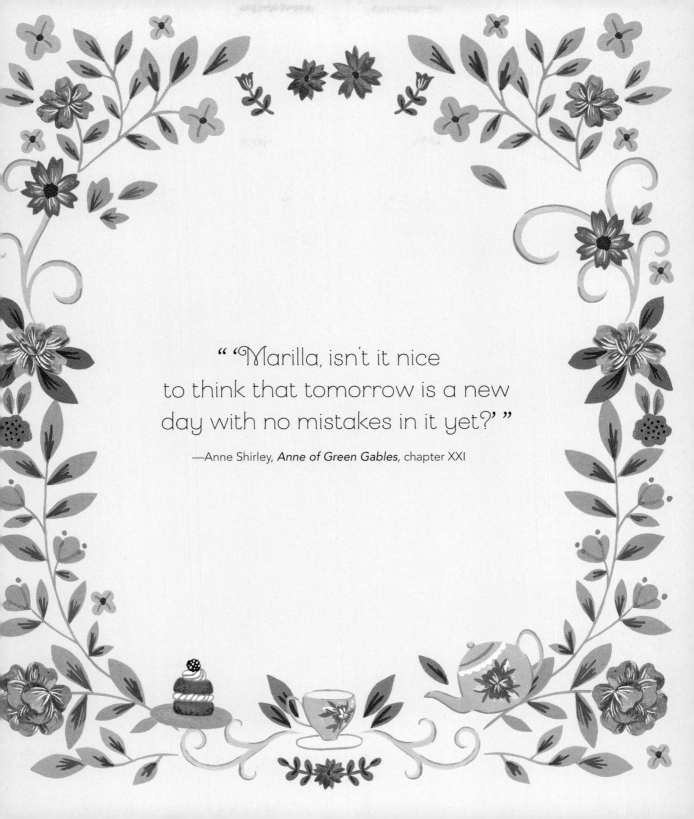

" "Marilla, isn't it nice
to think that tomorrow is a new
day with no mistakes in it yet?" "

—Anne Shirley, *Anne of Green Gables,* chapter XXI

Miss Stacy's **BAKED MACARONI**

—

Prep time: 40 minutes **Total time:** 1 hour 10 minutes **Yield:** serves 2 as a main and 4 as a side

> " 'I love Miss Stacy with my whole heart, Marilla. She is so ladylike and she has such a sweet voice. When she pronounces my name, I feel instinctively she's spelling it with an E.' "
>
> —Anne Shirley, CHAPTER XXIV

INGREDIENTS

1 tablespoon (15 g) butter, plus more for greasing
1 cup (105 g) elbow macaroni
1 tablespoon (8 g) all-purpose flour
1 cup (235 ml) 2% milk
1 cup (120 g) grated Cheddar cheese, divided
½ teaspoon salt
Black pepper, to taste
¼ teaspoon paprika

You Will Need
- Small casserole or baking dish

1. Preheat the oven to 350°F (180°C). Grease a small casserole dish with butter.

2. Bring a medium saucepan of salted water to a boil. Add the macaroni noodles and cook until tender. Drain the noodles in a colander and rinse under cold water. Set aside.

3. In a different medium saucepan, melt the butter over medium heat, then add the flour. When the flour is mixed in, add the milk.

4. Add ¾ cup (90 g) of the grated cheese and cook and stir until the cheese melts. Stir in the salt, black pepper, and paprika. Remove from the heat.

5. Add the cooked noodles to the greased casserole dish and mix in the cheese sauce.

6. Top with the remaining ¼ cup (30 g) cheese and bake for 30 minutes. Use oven mitts to remove the dish from the oven.

7. Serve immediately.

Afternoon **RUBY TEA BISCUITS**

—

Prep time: 35 minutes **Total time:** 50 minutes **Yield:** 12 tea biscuits

> "Mrs. Rachel and Marilla sat comfortably in the parlor while Anne got the tea and made hot biscuits that were light and white enough to defy even Mrs. Rachel's criticism."
>
> **—CHAPTER XXX**

INGREDIENTS

2 cups (220 g) sifted all-purpose flour, plus more for the work surface and rolling pin
4 teaspoons baking powder
2 tablespoons (30 ml) sugar
½ teaspoon salt
½ cup (95 g) vegetable shortening
¾ cup (180 ml) milk
½ cup (160 g) red jam or jelly

You Will Need
• Rolling pin
• Biscuit cutters (1 large and 1 small)

1. Preheat the oven to 425°F (220°C).

2. Add the sifted flour, baking powder, sugar, and salt, and mix with a fork in a large mixing bowl.

3. With a pastry blender, cut in the vegetable shortening until the mixture looks like coarse bread crumbs.

4. Add the milk and mix it into the flour with the fork, until the mixture forms a soft ball.

5. Place the ball of dough on a lightly floured surface and knead it 12 times.

6. Rub some flour onto a rolling pin and roll out the dough until it's about ¼ inch (6 mm) thick.

7. With a large biscuit cutter, cut circles, very close to-gether, in the dough. Use a straight downward motion, and don't twist the cutter.

8. With a metal spatula, lift *half* of the circles, one at a time, onto an ungreased cookie sheet. Arrange them about 1 inch (2.5 cm) apart.

9. With a small biscuit cutter, cut a hole in the remaining half of the circles to make rings, and lift out the centers with the spatula. Set these little centers aside. (With the leftover centers of dough, you could bake some little plain biscuits.)

 continued

10. With the spatula, place the rings on top of the large circles on the cookie sheet.

11. Put a teaspoonful of jam or jelly in the middle of each ring.

12. Bake the biscuits for 12 to 15 minutes, or until puffed and slightly golden.

13. Use oven mitts to remove the cookie sheet from the oven. Immediately lift the tea biscuits from the cookie sheet with the metal spatula.

14. Serve them either warm or cool.

White Sands SCALLOPED TOMATOES

—

Prep time: 20 minutes **Total time:** 50 minutes **Yield:** 6 to 8 servings

> "Anne was dressing for a concert at the White Sands Hotel. . . . As Anne would have said at one time, 'it was an epoch in her life,' and she was deliciously athrill with the excitement of it."
>
> **—CHAPTER XXXIII**

INGREDIENTS

3 tablespoons (45 g) butter, plus more for greasing and dotting
1 cup (60 g) fresh bread crumbs
1 teaspoon salt
Black pepper, to taste
1 tablespoon (10 g) grated onion
1 tablespoon (13 g) sugar
6 large tomatoes

You Will Need
• 9 x 13-inch (23 x 33 cm) baking pan

1. Preheat the oven to 350°F (180°C). Grease a 9 x 13-inch (23 x 33 cm) baking pan with butter. Set it aside.

2. In a medium microwave-safe bowl, melt the butter in a microwave. Add the breadcrumbs, salt, black pepper, onion, and sugar to the melted butter. Mix well.

3. With a sharp knife, slice the tomatoes into ½-inch-thick (13 mm) slices.

4. Add about one-third of the breadcrumb mixture to the bottom of the greased baking pan.

5. Add a layer of tomatoes, another layer of bread-crumbs, and another layer of tomatoes, and top with the remaining bread crumbs.

6. Dot a little butter here and there on top.

7. Bake for 30 minutes, or until a little golden on top. Use oven mitts to remove the pan from the oven.

8. Serve immediately.

Matthew Cuthbert's YUMMY BISCUIT SANDWICH

Prep time: 25 minutes **Total time:** 45 minutes **Yield:** 8 biscuit sandwiches

" 'Oh, Anne, I know I've been kind of strict and harsh with you maybe—but you mustn't think I didn't love you as well as Matthew did, for all that.' "

—Marilla Cuthbert, CHAPTER XXXVII

INGREDIENTS

2 cups (240 g) all-purpose flour, plus more for the work surface and rolling pin
4 teaspoons baking powder
1 teaspoon salt
3 tablespoons (36 g) vegetable shortening
¾ cup (180 ml) 2% milk
Butter, for spreading
8 lettuce leaves
2 large tomatoes, sliced
8 strips cooked bacon
Condiments such as Cavendish Catsup (page 98), mayonnaise, mustard, etc.

1. Preheat the oven to 450°F (230°C).

2. Sift the flour, baking powder, and salt together into a large mixing bowl.

3. Rub the shortening into the flour mixture with your fingers until it is well distributed. Stir in the milk.

4. Turn the dough out onto a floured board or countertop. Flour a rolling pin and roll out the dough until it is 1 inch (2.5 cm) thick.

5. With the rim of a large drinking glass, cut the dough into 8 rounds and place them 1 inch (2.5 cm) apart on an ungreased baking sheet.

6. Bake for 12 to 15 minutes until golden brown. Use oven mitts to remove the baking sheet from the oven.

7. Split the biscuits while hot and butter both halves lightly.

8. Place a lettuce leaf, a couple of tomato slices, and a strip of bacon on each biscuit half and cover with the other half.

9. Serve hot with Cavendish Catsup or your favorite condiments.

RECIPES FROM
Anne
of Avonlea

Davy and Dora's **MONKEY FACES**

Prep time: 25 minutes **Total time:** 45 minutes **Yield:** 24 monkey faces

> " 'Dear me, it doesn't seem
> a day since poor Matthew
> brought Anne herself home and
> everybody laughed at the idea
> of Marilla bringing up a child.
> And now she has adopted twins.
> You're never safe from being
> surprised till you're dead.' "

—Mrs. Rachel Lynde, CHAPTER VIII

INGREDIENTS

¼ cup (½ stick, or 60 g) butter, plus more
    for greasing
½ cup (100 g) sugar
1 large egg, beaten
½ cup (170 g) molasses
1 teaspoon baking soda
1½ cups (180 g) all-purpose flour
½ teaspoon ground cinnamon
½ teaspoon ground cloves
⅛ teaspoon salt
Raisins, for decorating

You Will Need
- 24-cup mini-muffin tin
- Electric mixer

1. Arrange the oven racks so that the pans will sit in the center of the oven. Preheat the oven to 375°F (190°C). Grease a 24-cup mini-muffin tin with butter.

2. Add the butter and sugar to a large mixing bowl, and cream together with an electric mixer. Mix in the beaten egg.

3. In a small bowl, add the molasses, then mix in the baking soda with a rubber spatula. Add this mixture to the creamed sugar, butter, and egg.

4. In a different large mixing bowl, sift together the flour, cinnamon, cloves, and salt.

5. Gradually add the flour mixture to the wet ingredients. Beat the mixture together well with an electric mixer.

6. Drop the mixture by the teaspoonful into the greased muffin tin.

7. Decorate each cookie with the raisins for the eyes and nose.

8. Bake for 15 to 18 minutes. Use oven mitts to remove the tin from the oven. Let the muffins cool in the tin for a few minutes before transferring them to a cooling rack so the bottoms don't turn soggy.

Poetical EGG SALAD SANDWICHES

—

Prep time: 50 minutes **Total time:** 50 minutes **Yield:** 8 sandwiches

> "The girls sat down by the roots and did full justice to Anne's dainties, even the unpoetical sandwiches being greatly appreciated by hearty, unspoiled appetites sharpened by all the fresh air and exercise they had enjoyed."
>
> **—CHAPTER XIII**

INGREDIENTS

4 large eggs
1 celery stalk, finely chopped
3 tablespoons (45 g) mayonnaise
½ teaspoon salt
Pinch black pepper
¼ cup (½ stick, or 60 g) butter, softened
2 tablespoons (30 ml) dried mint or
   parsley
8 slices fresh bread

1. Place the eggs in a small saucepan and cover them with cold water, at least 1 inch (2.5 cm) above the eggs. Bring to a boil.

2. Remove the saucepan from the heat and cover it. Let the eggs stand in the hot water for 25 minutes. Uncover the saucepan and place it under cold running water for 10 minutes to cool the eggs.

3. Peel the eggs, then add them, with the chopped celery, to a small mixing bowl. Mash them together with a fork.

4. Stir the mayonnaise, salt, and black pepper into the egg mixture. Place the egg salad in the refrigerator.

5. Mix the softened butter with the dried mint or parsley in a small bowl.

6. Butter one side of each slice of bread with the herb butter. Spread the egg salad on 4 of the bread slices and top with the buttered slices of bread.

7. Slice each sandwich in half diagonally.

Old-Fashioned **LEMONADE**

—

Prep time: 20 minutes **Total time:** 50 minutes (includes cooling) **Yield:** 3½ cups (820 ml) lemonade syrup

> "Anne had brought glasses and lemonade for her guests, but for her own part drank cold brook water from a cup fashioned out of birch bark. . . . Anne thought it more appropriate to the occasion than lemonade."
>
> **—CHAPTER XIII**

INGREDIENTS

1½ cups (250 g) sugar
1½ cups (350 ml) water
Finely grated peel of 1 lemon
1½ cups (350 ml) lemon juice
½ cup (120 ml) grenadine syrup (optional)
Ice cubes, for serving
Lemon slices, for serving
Fresh mint leaves, for serving (optional)

1. Add the sugar, water, and finely grated lemon peel to a large saucepan.

2. While stirring constantly with a wooden spoon, bring the mixture to a boil for 5 minutes. Remove the saucepan from the stove and let the mixture cool.

3. Add the lemon juice to the mixture.

4. Pour the lemonade syrup into a 1-quart (1 L) jar and cover it tightly with the lid. (For pink lemonade, add the grenadine syrup to the jar and shake.) The syrup can be kept in the refrigerator for 2 to 3 weeks.

5. When you're ready to serve the lemonade, put 2 ice cubes in the bottom of each glass. Pour ¼ cup (60 ml) lemonade syrup over the ice cubes. Add ¾ cup (180 ml) cold water and stir.

6. Float a thin slice of lemon and a fresh mint leaf, if using, in each glass.

Splendid LETTUCE SALAD

—

Prep time: 50 minutes **Total time:** 50 minutes **Yield:** 4 servings

" 'Oh, Anne, mayn't I help you cook the dinner?' implored Diana. 'You know I can make splendid lettuce salad.' "

—Diana Barry, CHAPTER XVI

INGREDIENTS

Thousand Island Dressing
1 large egg
1 cup (240 g) mayonnaise
¼ cup (60 g) 2% milk
2 tablespoons (30 g) ketchup
2 tablespoons (30 g) green pickle relish
1 tablespoon (10 g) chopped green pepper
1 tablespoon (15 ml) dehydrated onion flakes

Splendid Lettuce Salad
2 small celery stalks, cut into bite-size pieces
1 small green pepper, cut into bite-size pieces
½ cucumber, cut into bite-size pieces
2 small tomatoes, cut into bite-size pieces
½ cup (50 g) white mushrooms, thinly sliced
½ small head iceberg lettuce, leaves separated
½ small bunch romaine lettuce, leaves separated
12 large spinach leaves, stems removed

1. **To make the thousand island dressing:** Place the egg in a small saucepan and cover it with cold water, at least 1 inch (2.5 cm) above the egg. Bring to a boil.

2. Remove the saucepan from the heat and cover it. Let the egg stand in the hot water for 25 minutes. Cool the egg under cold running water and peel it.

3. With a fork, mash the hard-boiled egg in a small mixing bowl. Add the mayonnaise, milk, ketchup, relish, green pepper, and onion flakes, and mix well with a wooden spoon. Set aside.

4. **To make the splendid lettuce salad:** Add the celery, green pepper, cucumber, tomatoes, and mushrooms to a large bowl.

5. Tear the lettuce leaves into bite-size pieces. Add the lettuce to the other vegetables and toss the salad with your hands—make sure they're clean!

6. Line a salad serving bowl with the spinach leaves so that they peek out around the edge. Mound the tossed salad in the middle.

7. Serve in individual bowls with a dollop of the Thousand Island Dressing.

Saucy CHICKEN

Prep time: 30 minutes **Total time:** 1 hour 30 minutes **Yield:** 4 to 6 servings

> "Then the girls tripped out to the kitchen, which was filled with appetizing odors emanating from the oven, where the chickens were already sizzling splendidly."
>
> **—CHAPTER XVII**

INGREDIENTS

2½ pounds (1 kg) chicken pieces
1 tablespoon (15 g) butter
1 small yellow onion, finely chopped
1 garlic clove, finely chopped
¼ cup (60 g) ketchup
¼ cup (60 ml) white vinegar
2 tablespoons (30 ml) lemon juice
1 tablespoon (15 ml) Worcestershire sauce
2 tablespoons (30 g) firmly packed brown sugar
1 teaspoon salt

You Will Need
• 9 x 3-inch (23 x 33 cm)
• Electric mixer

This chicken is great when cooked on the grill, too!

1. Preheat the oven to 375°F (190°C).

2. Pull off any large lumps of fat from the chicken pieces. Arrange the chicken pieces in a 9 x 13-inch (23 x 33 cm) baking dish and bake them for 40 minutes.

3. While the chicken bakes, melt the butter in a small saucepan. Add the onion and garlic, and cook over low heat until the onion is transparent, about 5 minutes.

4. Stir in the ketchup, vinegar, lemon juice, Worcestershire sauce, brown sugar, and salt. Mix with a wooden spoon.

5. Bring the sauce to a boil, then reduce the heat to low and simmer for 10 minutes. Remove from the heat.

6. Use oven mitts to remove the baking dish from the oven. Spoon half the sauce over the chicken and put it back in the oven for 10 minutes.

7. Remove the chicken from the oven again. With tongs, turn the chicken pieces over. Spoon the rest of the sauce on top and bake for another 10 minutes.

8. Serve immediately. Pair with the Splendid Lettuce Salad (page 69), if desired.

Thick and Creamy VEGETABLE SOUP

—

Prep time: 1 hour **Total time:** 1 hour **Yield:** 4 to 6 servings

"One o'clock came . . .
but no Priscilla or Mrs. Morgan.
Anne was in an agony. Everything
was done to a turn and the soup
was just what soup should be, but
couldn't be depended on to remain
so for any length of time."

—CHAPTER XVII

INGREDIENTS

2 tablespoons (30 g) butter
2 small yellow onions, finely chopped
2 large celery stalks, finely chopped
1 cup (180 g) canned diced tomatoes, drained,
   or 3 small tomatoes, diced
1 teaspoon salt
Pinch black pepper
1 teaspoon dried basil leaves
1 tablespoon (15 ml) dried parsley
2 cups (475 ml) chicken broth or 2 chicken cubes
   plus 2 cups (475 ml) boiling water
2 medium carrots, peeled and diced
1 large potato or 2 small ones, peeled and diced
½ cup (75 g) frozen peas
2½ cups (600 ml) 2% milk
1 green onion, sliced, for topping

You Will Need
• blender

1. Add the butter and chopped onion and celery to a large saucepan. Cook and stir over low heat until the vegetables are soft, 5 to 7 minutes.

2. Add the tomatoes to a large mixing bowl. Add the salt, black pepper, basil, and parsley. Mash the tomatoes and seasonings a bit with a wooden spoon.

3. When the onions and celery are soft, add the chicken broth to the saucepan. Add the carrots, potatoes, peas, and tomatoes, and mix together with the wooden spoon.

4. Bring the soup to a boil. Reduce the heat to medium. Boil gently to cook the vegetables, about 15 minutes.

5. Pour the soup into a large mixing bowl. Ladle half of the soup into a blender and blend on low speed until very smooth. Pour the pureed soup back into the saucepan. Blend the other half of the soup and pour it into the saucepan. Stir in the milk.

6. Heat over medium heat, just until the milk is hot, about 7 minutes. Don't let it boil.

7. Ladle the soup into bowls and sprinkle green onion over the top.

Cowcumber **BOATS**

—

Prep time: 50 minutes **Total time:** 50 minutes **Yield:** 6 boats

" 'You must be real tired and
hungry. I'll do the best I can
for you in the way of tea but I
warn you not to expect anything
but bread and butter and
some cowcumbers.' "

—**Miss Sarah Copp, CHAPTER XVIII**

INGREDIENTS

3 cups (700 ml) water
Pinch plus ½ teaspoon salt, divided
⅓ cup (35 g) elbow macaroni
7 ounces (198 g) canned tuna, drained
1 medium carrot, peeled and grated
1 medium celery stalk, finely chopped
⅓ cup (80 g) mayonnaise
2 tablespoons (30 ml) lemon juice
Pinch black pepper
3 medium cucumbers
1 tablespoon (4 g) chopped parsley,
   for topping (optional)

Many years ago cucumbers were called
"cowcumbers"—probably because this was
the English way of pronouncing the old French
word *coucombre*.

1. Add the water and a pinch of salt to a small saucepan.
   Bring to a boil. Add the elbow macaroni gradually and
   boil until tender, 8 to 10 minutes. Drain the macaroni in
   a colander and transfer it to a medium mixing bowl.

2. Add the tuna to the macaroni. Add the carrot and celery
   to the macaroni and tuna.

3. Add the mayonnaise, lemon juice, ½ teaspoon salt, and
   black pepper to the bowl and combine with a fork. Set
   aside.

4. Peel the cucumbers with a vegetable peeler and trim
   the ends. Cut each cucumber in half, lengthwise. With a
   large spoon, scoop out and discard the seeds and any
   watery flesh.

5. Fill each cucumber boat with the tuna mixture.

6. Sprinkle the boats with the parsley, if using.

Mrs. Irving's DELICIOUS SHORTBREAD

Prep time: 45 minutes **Total time:** 1 hour 30 minutes **Yield:** 36 cookies

> " 'Of course I'll stay to tea,'
> said Anne gaily. 'I was dying to
> be asked. My mouth has been
> watering for some more of
> your grandma's delicious
> shortbread ever since I had
> tea here before.' "
>
> **—CHAPTER XIX**

INGREDIENTS

1 cup (2 sticks, or 240 g) butter, softened
½ cup (60 g) confectioners' sugar
2 cups (240 g) all-purpose flour, plus more
   for the work surface and rolling pin
Pinch salt
¼ teaspoon baking powder
Granulated sugar, for sprinkling

You Will Need
- Electric mixer
- Rolling pin
- Cookie cutters

1. Preheat the oven to 350°F (180°C).

2. With an electric mixer, cream the butter in a large mixing bowl until it is soft, smooth, and fluffy. Add the confectioners' sugar, a little at a time, and beat until smooth.

3. Add the flour, salt, and baking powder to a medium mixing bowl. Combine with a fork.

4. Add the flour mixture to the butter mixture and stir until well combined.

5. Turn the dough out onto a lightly floured board or countertop. Flour a rolling pin and roll the dough out, about ¼ inch (6 mm) thick.

6. With cookie cutters of any shape, cut out the dough. Reroll the remaining dough and continue cutting until all is used.

7. With a metal spatula, lift the shortbreads onto an ungreased cookie sheet. Place them about ½ inch (13 mm) apart. Prick each shortbread twice with a fork and sprinkle with granulated sugar.

8. Bake the shortbreads for 15 to 20 minutes, until they turn light brown around the edges.

9. Use oven mitts to remove the cookie sheet from the oven. With the metal spatula, immediately lift the shortbreads onto a plate. Serve warm or cool.

Creamy **BUTTERSCOTCH PUDDING**

—

Prep time: 30 minutes **Total time:** 1 hour 30 minutes (includes cooling) **Yield:** 4 to 6 servings

" 'I wish people could live on pudding. Why can't they, Marilla? I want to know.' "

—Davy Keith, CHAPTER XXVII

INGREDIENTS

2 eggs
1 cup (225 g) firmly packed brown sugar
2 tablespoons (30 ml) cornstarch
¼ teaspoon salt
2 cups (475 ml) milk
2 tablespoons (30 g) butter
1 teaspoon vanilla extract
Whipped cream, for serving (optional)

1. Break the eggs and separate the yolks and whites into 2 small bowls. Beat the yolks with the fork and set them aside. (You can use the whites in a different recipe or discard.)

2. Combine the brown sugar, cornstarch, and salt in a medium saucepan. With a wooden spoon, gradually stir in the milk.

3. Place the saucepan over medium heat. Cook and stir the mixture until it is thick and bubbling, 10 to 15 minutes. Stir and cook for 2 more minutes, then remove the saucepan off the heat.

4. Dip a measuring cup into the hot mixture and take out about 1 cup (235 ml). Very slowly stir the cup of hot mixture into the egg yolks, then stir the hot egg-yolk mixture into a large saucepan. Stirring constantly, cook over medium heat for 2 more minutes.

5. Remove the saucepan from the heat and add the butter and vanilla extract. Stir with the wooden spoon until the butter melts.

6. Pour the pudding into a serving bowl. To keep a skin from forming on top, carefully place a piece of plastic wrap over the hot pudding and chill in the refrigerator, about 1 hour.

7. When ready to serve, remove the plastic wrap and spoon the pudding into small bowls. Top with whipped cream, if desired.

RECIPES FROM
Anne of
Windy Poplars

Miss Ellen's POUND CAKE

—

Prep time: 15 minutes **Total time:** 1 hour 30 minutes **Yield:** 5 x 9-inch (13 x 23 cm) loaf

> " 'I wish I could get Miss Ellen's recipe for pound cake,' sighed Aunt Chatty. 'She's promised it to me time and again but it never comes. It's an old English family recipe. They're so exclusive about their recipes.' "

—THE FIRST YEAR, CHAPTER II

INGREDIENTS

1 cup (2 sticks, or 240 g) butter, softened, plus more for greasing
1¾ cups (210 g) all-purpose flour, plus more for the pan
1½ cups (250 g) granulated sugar
6 large eggs
1 teaspoon vanilla extract
½ teaspoon salt

You Will Need
- 5 x 9-inch (13 x 23 cm) loaf pan
- Electric mixer

It's called "pound cake" because all the ingredients used to be added in one-pound quantities. This version is more practical.

1. Preheat the oven to 325°F (170°C). Grease a 5 x 9-inch (13 x 23 cm) loaf pan with butter, then flour it.

2. With an electric mixer, cream the butter in a large mixing bowl until soft, smooth, and fluffy. Add the sugar, a little at a time, beating until light and fluffy.

3. Add the eggs, one at a time. Beat well after adding each egg. Mix in the vanilla extract.

4. With a wooden spoon, stir in the flour and salt. Mix well.

5. Pour the batter into the loaf pan. Smooth the top with a spatula and bake the cake for 75 to 90 minutes.

6. Test the cake with a toothpick. If it isn't done, test again in 15 minutes. Use oven mitts to remove the pan from the oven. Let the cake cool in the pan for 10 minutes.

7. Slide the blade of a metal spatula around the edges of the cake to loosen it from the pan. Turn the cake upside down on a cooling rack and gently lift off the loaf pan. Let it cool completely.

8. To serve, cut the pound cake into thin slices with a bread knife.

Coconut **MACAROONS**

Prep time: 15 minutes **Total time:** 1 hour 15 minutes (includes cooling) **Yield:** 18 macaroons

> " 'No, thank you, Kate, I won't have any more tea . . . well, mebbe a macaroon. They don't lie heavy on the stomach, but I'm afraid I've et far too much.' "
>
> **—Cousin Ernestine Bugle,**
> **THE SECOND YEAR, CHAPTER VIII**

INGREDIENTS

3 large eggs, room temperature
¼ teaspoon cream of tartar
¾ cup (90 g) confectioners' sugar
2 cups (190 g) shredded sweetened coconut
½ teaspoon almond extract

You Will Need
- Electric mixer

1. Preheat the oven to 300°F (150°C). Line a cookie sheet with parchment paper or a silicone baking mat.

2. Break the eggs and separate them, putting the yolks in a small bowl and the whites in a large bowl. Beat the whites with an electric mixer until foamy. Add the cream of tartar and beat until the egg whites are stiff and glossy but not dry. (You can use the egg yolks in another recipe.)

3. With a rubber spatula, carefully fold the confectioners' sugar, coconut, and almond extract into the egg whites. Do not stir.

4. Drop the batter by teaspoonfuls onto the prepared cookie sheet, about 1 inch (2.5 cm) apart. Bake the macaroons for 30 to 35 minutes, until they look dry on top.

5. Use oven mitts to remove the cookie sheet from the oven. Dampen a tea towel and lay it on the counter. Lift the brown paper and macaroons onto the tea towel. Let them cool completely. Peel the macaroons off the parchment paper or baking mat and put them on a plate.

Orange ANGEL CAKE

Prep time: 35 minutes **Total time:** 2 hours 30 minutes (includes cooling and glazing) **Yield:** 10-inch (25 cm) cake

> " 'Rebecca Dew has been making all my favorite dishes for a week now . . . she even devoted ten eggs to angel-cake *twice* . . . and using the "company" china.' "
>
> —Anne Shirley,
> **THE THIRD YEAR, CHAPTER XIV**

INGREDIENTS

Angel Cake

1 cup (120 g) all-purpose flour
½ cup (60 g) confectioners' sugar
½ teaspoon salt
10 or 11 eggs, room temperature
1 teaspoon vanilla extract
1 teaspoon orange extract
1 tablespoon (6 g) finely grated orange peel
1½ teaspoons cream of tartar
1 cup (200 g) granulated sugar

1. Arrange the oven racks so the cake will sit near the bottom. Preheat the oven to 350°F (180°C).

2. **To make the cake:** Sift the flour onto a piece of wax paper. Measure out 1 cup (110 g) and put it back into the sifter. Add the confectioners' sugar and salt to the sifter. Sift onto another piece of wax paper. Sift again 4 more times, and set aside.

3. Break the eggs and separate them, putting the yolks in a small bowl and the egg whites into a medium bowl. Make sure there is no yolk in the whites. (You can use the yolks in other recipes or discard.) Measure the egg whites for 1½ cups (365 g) and add them to a large mixing bowl. Add the vanilla extract, orange extract, and orange peel to the egg whites.

4. Beat the egg whites with an electric mixer until they are foamy. Add the cream of tartar and continue beating until the egg whites are firm but still glossy.

5. Add the granulated sugar, 2 tablespoons (25 g) at a time, to the egg whites. Continue beating until they cling to the sides of the bowl and are stiff but not dry.

6. With a rubber spatula, fold in the sifted flour and confectioners' sugar a little at a time. Do not stir.

 continued

RECIPES FROM
L.M. Montgomery's Kitchen

Rachel Lynde's NORTH SHORE FISH CAKES

—

Prep time: 30 minutes **Total time:** 1 hour 15 minutes **Yield:** 8 fish cakes

There are many reasons to visit Prince Edward Island: seafood, the beautiful beaches, secret coves, red sandstone formations, and of course, the fictional home of *Anne of Green Gables*.

INGREDIENTS

Mashed Potatoes

2 or 3 large Yukon Gold potatoes (for 2 cups, or 450 g, mashed potatoes)
2 tablespoons (30 g) butter
¼ cup (60 ml) 2% milk

Fish Cakes

1 or 2 cod or haddock fillets (for 2 cups, or 400 g, cooked fish)
Water
2 eggs
1 small onion, minced
1 tablespoon (15 ml) Dijon mustard
Salt, to taste
Black pepper, to taste
½ cup (30 g) fresh bread crumbs
1 to 2 tablespoons vegetable oil (15 to 30 ml) or butter (15 to 30 g), for frying
Lemon wedges, for serving

1. **To make the mashed potatoes:** Peel and cut the potatoes into small pieces. Boil the potatoes in a medium saucepan filled with salted water. When you can insert a fork easily into the potatoes, they're done. Drain off the water, then add the butter and milk to the saucepan. Mash with a potato masher. Set aside.

2. **To make the fish cakes:** Add the fish to a medium frying pan and add enough water to cover the fillets. Poach the fish until it flakes with a fork. Drain off the water and mash the fish. Add the fish to the mashed potatoes. Combine.

3. Break the eggs into a small bowl. Add the eggs, minced onion, Dijon, salt, and black pepper to the potatoes and fish. Combine all the ingredients.

4. Form the mixture into cakes about the size of a hockey puck.

5. Spread the bread crumbs on a baking sheet, then coat both sides of each fish cake with them.

6. Add the vegetable oil to a large frying pan and fry the fish cakes to a nice golden brown.

7. Serve immediately with the lemon wedges.

Fire and Dew SWEET POTATOES

Prep time: 10 minutes **Total time:** 1 hour 10 minutes **Yield:** 4 servings

"The good stars met in your horoscope, Made you of spirit and fire and dew—"

"EVELYN HOPE" BY ROBERT BROWNING, A FAVORITE POET OF L.M. MONTGOMERY

INGREDIENTS
2 good-size sweet potatoes
1 tablespoon (15 g) butter, plus more for brushing and topping
2 tablespoons (30 ml) 2% milk
1 egg, beaten
Salt, to taste
Black pepper, to taste

1. Preheat the oven to 400°F (200°C).

2. Scrub the sweet potatoes and place on a baking sheet. Bake in the oven until they are soft when squeezed, about 40 minutes. Use oven mitts to remove the potatoes from the oven. Don't turn off the oven.

3. Halve the potatoes lengthwise.

4. Scoop out the flesh, keeping the skins intact, and put it in a small bowl. Reserve the skins. Add the butter and milk to the flesh. Mix well. Fold in the beaten egg and season with salt and black pepper.

5. Pack the mixture back into the reserved skins, place them on a baking sheet, and brush the tops with a little butter.

6. Bake for 15 to 20 minutes, until heated through and a little brown on top.

7. Serve immediately, with a little butter on top.

Green Gables SHEPHERD'S PIE

—

Prep time: 15 minutes **Total time:** 1 hour 30 minutes **Yield:** 4 to 6 servings

In the olden days, this dish was made using leftover roasted meat. It's called Shepherd's Pie because it was originally made from lamb which was affordable for the rural workers who tended to the sheep.

INGREDIENTS

4 medium Yukon Gold potatoes
1 tablespoon (15 g) butter, plus more for dotting
2 tablespoons (30 ml) 2% milk
1 tablespoon (15 ml) vegetable oil
2 medium onions, chopped
1 pound (454 g) ground beef
1 teaspoon Worcestershire sauce
Beef stock cube and water
2 tablespoons gravy thickener (such as Knorr or McCormick brand) or Bisto
¼ cup (60 ml) cold water
1 cup (225 g) frozen mixed vegetables
Salt, to taste
Black pepper, to taste

You Will Need
- 1½-quart (1.5 L) baking or casserole dish

1. Preheat the oven to 350°F (180°C).

2. Peel and cut the potatoes into small pieces. Boil the potatoes in a medium saucepan filled with salted water. When you can insert a fork easily into the potatoes, they're done. Drain off the water, then add the butter and milk to the saucepan. Mash with a potato masher. Set aside.

3. Heat the vegetable oil in a large frying pan. Add the onions and cook and stir until soft. Add the ground beef, breaking it up with a wooden spoon. Cook until the beef is brown. Stir in the Worcestershire sauce.

4. To make some gravy, add the beef stock cube and required water, according to the package instructions, to the meat. Cook for 15 minutes.

5. In a small bowl, mix together the gravy thickener and cold wate. Add gradually to the frying pan with the hot meat, while stirring, until it thickens.

6. Add the frozen vegetables and season with salt and black pepper. Combine.

7. Drain off the extra gravy from the pan and reserve.

8. Transfer the meat mixture to a 1½-quart (1.5 L) baking dish and spread the mashed potatoes on top. Dot a little butter here and there on the potatoes and bake for 30 minutes. Use oven mitts to remove the dish from the oven.

9. Serve immediately with the reserved gravy.

Cavendish CATSUP

—

Prep time: 20 minutes **Total time:** 2 hours **Yield:** 2½ cups (360 g)

The town of Avonlea in the *Anne of Green Gables* books is based on L.M. Montgomery's childhood home of Cavendish, a beautiful pastoral community on the north shore of Prince Edward Island.

INGREDIENTS

12 plum or small tomatoes
1 small onion, minced
¾ cup (170 g) firmly packed brown sugar
1 cup (235 ml) white vinegar
1 tablespoon (15 ml) salt
½ teaspoon dry mustard
1 teaspoon ground cinnamon
½ teaspoon paprika

1. Bring a medium saucepan of water to a boil. On the bottom of each tomato make an X with a sharp paring knife.

2. Dunk each tomato into the boiling water for about 30 seconds, until you can see that the skin is coming away from the tomato. Use a slotted spoon and dunk each tomato individually. Set them aside on a cutting board to cool.

3. Peel the cooled tomatoes, then chop them into small pieces.

4. Add the onion, brown sugar, vinegar, salt, mustard cinnamon, and paprika to a medium saucepan. Bring the mixture to a boil, then reduce the heat to a simmer for about 1 hour, until the mixture is reduced in half.

5. Remove from the heat and let cool.

6. Serve with Mathew Cuthbert's Yummy Biscuit Sandwich (page 59); see catsup in that photo for reference)

7. Store in an airtight container in the refrigerator for up to 8 weeks.

Acknowledgments

I would like to extend my heartfelt thanks to Sally Keefe Cohen for all her efforts and help in making this book a reality. I'd also like to extend my gratitude to Jeannine Dillon and the team at Race Point Publishing, including Erin Canning, Merideth Harte, and Jen Cogliantry. Lastly, I would like to thank photographer Evi Abeler and food stylist Michaela Hayes for making the food of *Anne of Green Gables* come to life on these pages.

About the Author

Photo Credit: Diane Trojan

With a college degree in food and nutrition, Kate Macdonald has a very special interest in *The Anne of Green Gables Cookbook*; she is one of L.M. Montgomery's grandchildren. Kate is the daughter of Ruth Macdonald and Dr. Stuart Macdonald who was L.M. Montgomery's youngest son.

Kate is the President of Heirs of L.M. Montgomery Inc., a family-owned company that oversees all L.M. Montgomery–related inquiries and projects. She is also a patron of the L.M. Montgomery Society of Ontario and on the boards of the L.M. Montgomery Heritage Society of Prince Edward Island and the Anne of Green Gables Licensing Authority Inc. She manages the Toronto office of the "Anne" Authority.

About L.M. Montgomery

L.M. (Lucy Maud) Montgomery (1874–1942) was born in Clifton (now New London), Prince Edward Island. Her mother died of tuberculosis when Montgomery was only twenty-one months old, leaving her in the care of her maternal grandparents in Cavendish.

Montgomery was an imaginative child who began writing poetry and keeping a journal at the age of nine. When she was sixteen, her first publication, a poem entitled "On Cape LeForce," was published in a Prince Edward Island newspaper. Montgomery went on to complete her coursework for a teacher's license from Prince of Wales College, graduating in one year instead of two, with honors.

Montgomery taught at three Prince Edward Island schools and took a year off from her teaching to attend Dalhousie University in Halifax, Nova Scotia, which was rare for a woman to do at that time. Montgomery's teaching career was cut short in 1898, when she moved back to Cavendish to care for her grandmother after her grandfather's death. While caring for her grandmother for thirteen years, Montgomery started making an income from her writing.

In 1905, she wrote Anne of Green Gables, but received several rejections from publishers. After putting the manuscript away for a couple years, she once again sought out a publisher and found success with the Page Company of Boston, Massachusetts, who published it with much acclaim in 1908.

After the death of her grandmother, Montgomery married the Reverend Ewan Macdonald in 1911, though they had been secretly engaged since 1906. Montgomery left Prince Edward Island for good, except for vacations, living in Ontario, where her husband's work as a Presbyterian minister took them. They had three sons: Chester (1912), Hugh (stillborn in 1914), and Stuart (1915). Montgomery continued to write over the years as she managed her household.

She is buried in the Cavendish cemetery on Prince Edward Island.

Opposite: L.M. Montgomery, in 1904, at thirty years of age.

INDEX

Page references in *italics* indicate photographs.

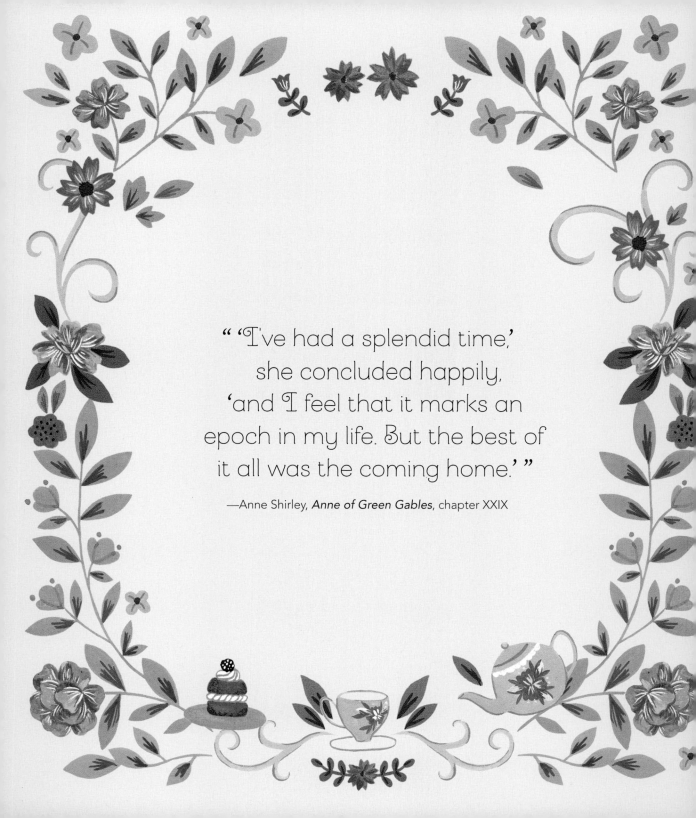

" 'I've had a splendid time,' she concluded happily, 'and I feel that it marks an epoch in my life. But the best of it all was the coming home.' "

—Anne Shirley, *Anne of Green Gables*, chapter XXIX